TREASURE HOUSE

SURABHI BHATTACHARJEE

ISBN 979-888521735-4

Contents

Contents

Preface

This book is a amalgamated form of different thoughts a collection book of 24 poems . Sometimes she is taking about love , relationship sometimes the same person is taking about hatred , revenge . And she is longing for vanquishing social dichotomy. A mysterious book where thoughts are going in different direction . Science fiction , Life mystery , and sometimes the author is becoming so close to nature. Magical , miraculous, supernatural phenomenon everything . So people will never get bored while reading this book .

Acknowledgements

I would like to say thanks to my acquaintance for encouraging me to write more . And I got inspiration from those people whom I admire a lot . And a special thanks to string publication house for publishing this book . And seeking blessing from everywhere for future journey . This is just the beginning long way to go .

About The Author

Surabhi Bhattacharjee

This book is a amalgamated form of different thoughts a collection book of 25 poems . Sometimes she is taking about love , relationship sometimes the same person is taking about hatred , revenge . And she is longing for vanquishing social dichotomy. A mysterious book where thoughts are going in different direction . Science fiction , Life mystery , and sometimes the author is becoming so close to nature. Magical , miraculous, supernatural phenomenon everything . So people will never get bored while reading this book .

CHAPTER ONE

ECCENTRICITY

Incoherent soul is thirsty
For knowing unknown, seeing unseen
Seeking new luminescence to see more;
Wants to get up everything passionately.

Doesn't want to believe majority
Wouldn't love to choose the path
Where everything is nebulous;
Wants to set the vision freely.

Quest appears like cruces
No longer rehabilitee
This soul is irrefutable;
People worried to assess.

Wandering soul has no vacation
Looking for solace
Where is the niche?
Yearn for solemnization.

CHAPTER TWO

Labyrinth

Deprived from the tenderness,
Always the receiver of detestation
Nature instills leniency in everyone;
But here rigidness appears.

Not so blessed,
Plummets from up to down
Unable to understand the labyrinth;
Still crawling and howling.

Encapsulated with deprivation,
Life is a labyrinth
All action radiates fruitions
Sunlight can't make it sensuous.

Longing for a miracle,
Let it be ambiguous
But still fallacious;
New chapter is coming up.

CHAPTER THREE

Alchemy

Insanity as its peak
Zest is stupendous;
Probably sanctified
Chasing something arduous.

Eyelashes are heavy,
Dreaming sustainably
Resonance is coming,
Flickering wings to fly high.

Crossing the limit
Beyond destination
In the parallel universe;
Enrich her with the power.

Catching a glimpse to observe,
Nihilism is calling;
OH universe!!
Instill a foray within her.

CHAPTER FOUR

The Hymnn of hope

I have seen
My tragic life;
How I had lost all the intuition
Thousand years old sanction?
How I buried myself?

My introspection was about to fade
When everyone was busy to manifest their own;
Culmination lies in variation,
My existence was completely depleted.
Suddenly hope appears,

A slugfest war is about to end.
Hope is the biggest threat here,
Challenging on and on
Now there is no entrance of despondent;
Always hope sustains life.

CHAPTER FIVE

Inked solace

Abbreviated desire peeping,
Like a murky light in dark;
Creating own fans
Defying boundaries.

Paradoxically time betraying,
Nightmare replacing fans;
Atrabilious rhythm
Banging out widely.

Luminous hollow stopping
Concoction contradicting factor;
Coherent fudge gestures
Something blooming out.
An unknown bard creates,
Own reminiscent album;
Obsession is keen
Smudge is still disappearing.

CHAPTER SIX

Intense proclivity

An unimpeachable beauty
Has driven me crazy.
That's unity has written history;
Trough golden words.
Hard to eradicate.

At the end of the day,
When people ask?
Who we are?
We just pass a smirk.
And say; We are Indians.

This intoxicated beauty,
Can easily demolish red wine;
Aching for a pulchritudinous one.
Hard to bid adieu,
Knot is in the name of obsession.

Celestial beauty lure me much,
An indigenous of India;
Wants to die willingly for nation.
My nation is stupendous;
Serves love ceaselessly to everyone.

CHAPTER SEVEN

Phenomenal victory

Who posits you like a slave?
Who dares to manipulate you?
Remember another conspiracy
You're tail spinning into the victimization.

You haven't born with all this
You asked to follow,
Don't fall for the trap
Dwindling is equal to death.

Break all the shackles and norms
Demands you to be inferior
You're above everything
Don't be someone's treasure.
Be gladiatorial, to unleash yourself
Don't open your heart everywhere,
Keep your inner storm alive
Use it to vandalize.

CHAPTER EIGHT

An Amaranthine Nightingale

A nightingale bird,
Is flattering wings to bring joy.
This nightingale is not enthralled,
Nightingale meant to be a heathen,

Nightingale is quite unconformity,
OH owl !! you're so fanatical.
You're so vindictive,
Nightingale is free and immoral.

OH, terrific owl!!fly away
Don't spoil Nightingale's song
Nightingale is the pioneer of new;
OH, orthodox owl! your time is over.

Nightingale is philistine,
Defying years old tradition.
Nightingale has an aversion attitude to culture
Nightingale has an inclination to rationale.

Nightingale is yearning for freedom,

Nightingale is not tethered.
Hitherto, no god has come across;
Nightingale refused to rely on.

CHAPTER NINE

Falling star

Every night I stay up,
Tell myself;
I am alright,
But feeling is perverse.

Sparkling stars are my company,
They know I have gone through many;
Every time I try to resuscitate myself,
Hogging for something solemn.

I have been seen,
Falling stars so many times, how they fall apart?
When the sky is all besets by sparkling stars?
It's hard to say adieu, ironically feeling is mutual.

I am self-dubious,
About the expected ideal paradigm;
I feel like thrown out,
Resolutely, I have hidden myself.

People think that's my propensity,
Nobody ever asked me;
What I want to be?

But wallflower also blooms.

CHAPTER TEN

Rebillious Doll

Doll is growing up
Crucial aspects are substantial;
Creative, magnificent, hell bent
Playing with her is dangerous.

Lack of lenient features
Can't be easily handed over
Seldom rebellious
Can easily bring destruction.

Freakiness running in her veins
Loving, caring;
As well as cruel and cold-hearted
Black represents her soul.

Scary eyes lovely smile
Talking through actions;
Augmented ambition is hell fire
Possessed by Annabelle; tit for tat.

CHAPTER ELEVEN

Wizard 's drama

Her wye speaks louder than words,
Thunder encourages her soul;
Mountain stands high in her ocean mind
Barefoot light in frozen land.

Thousands untold stories,
Grabbed her entity;
She sheds pearls
Through her tears.

The grace of sun,
She carries within her;
Crystal ball, magical wand
Ignited candle in the full moon night.
There is symphony,
Cynically lunatic;
She dances through the fire
Wizardly cacophony invokes Euphoric.

CHAPTER TWELVE

Moon Magic

Moon is mystic
The phases of moon
Resemble magical soul
Which we can't conclude.

Hoarded magical resource
Adequately breathtaking
Semi – transparent soul
Let it be exposed.

Resonance diplomacy
Glut of fairies
Camouflage and the secrecy of phases:
Maiden, Mother and crone.
Power is invincible
When everything is covered up
The Goddess walks
She invokes the new repercussions.

CHAPTER THIRTEEN

The Death Bell

OH volcano!!
Something in you must to blow
No never !! pour some fuel into the fire,
Unwanted rain doesn't hit here.

Lounge and the sword the relation is too old,
Language, power, and identity rule together.
Shield is devoted in the name of her beliefs,
She walks through the fire.

Knowledge is the weapon
Acrid soul, pungent vocal;
Very complicated life
Where folks feel screwed up.

She prefers to know herself first,
No time for love
Show to mess with her!!
Her venomous soul, poisonous stings all yours.

The perishable one is coming up,
Being vulnerable is the only chosen option.
You're near to your deathbed,

Destruction is ringing the bell.

CHAPTER FOURTEEN

Intimacy

Heavenly knot is tied up,
Finally, the day has come;
The universe fetched two souls together,
When sea and river meet?

Moon, star, wind, sky
Are the testimony of that moment,
When two souls meet?
When two souls become one?

That romantic moment
When one holds another's body?
Like waves flow in very rapid motion
Every touch has a magical vibe.

When bud starts blooming;
When drought place soak
The first drop of rain?
That becomes living proof.

CHAPTER FIFTEEN

Psychic Love

I am not just a ripple,
I can drown you away;
I am the holy fire,
Who will burn you into ashes;
And take you away very far over the sky.

Our thoughts will be amalgamated,
No ifs and buts;
Only perfection,
Acceptation without regression;
You're no longer an absconder.

When cupid hits us,
We might not catch evil eyes;
When love calls,
Everything will be miraculous;
I will catch you, you can't flinch anywhere.

Maybe I am as crazy as Betsy bugs,
You're as strident as hell;
Don't try to ditch me,
How it would be?
When we both will write a freaken love story?

CHAPTER SIXTEEN

Infinite Eternity

It seems like an accumulated curse of thousand years
People are grinding teeth with angers
Holding a venomous grudge
There's 100 little time to measure.

I'll forever be haunted by the pain
I choose to bury too early
Sprawling hatred makes a castle on the sea shore
Terminating love counts last breath.

I yearn a charismatic love
That would make the ocean,
Without any innovations
None is allowed to make puddle.

I want to go there
Where the sun doesn't set
A place where time doesn't exist
The place where the sun and moon meet.

Where love knee a carpet simultaneously
And where love leads over spirituality.
There is nothing left to discuss

Where people get drowned into intoxicated love.

CHAPTER SEVENTEEN

Be Unstoppable

I know;
You're dreaming, lying on your bed
Feeling unworthy of yourself
But your hope lends worth
Chase your dream and go ahead.

I can see;
You're trying but not getting success
It's ok, try again
One day you can access.

I know;
You've been hiring, you've been firing
But don't get depressed
Just deal savagely with your own way of going.

I can see;
You're facing darkness
Try to understand
It's Almighty's highness.

I heard;
They're saying continuously

It's not your cup of tea
You should cut them off relentlessly.

Be unstoppable!!
A bunch of people
mocking you today
But don't get baffled
The universe will present you a gala day.

I can assume;
There are plenty of negativity
To destroy
Your God made destiny.

It's the ultimate war of God versus Evil
And who you choose to pick the win
Only He shall
Control your power of will.

Set your soul on fire
Burn them with your igneous motion
And remember you're the dormant volcano
Waiting for the eruption.

CHAPTER EIGHTEEN

Inexplicable Life

I want to go on living,
Even after my death;
I rise from the ashes
Like a phoenix.

I will be invincible always,
Show to stop my reign;
I never stop
From growing.

Nobody can stop me,
To think, to create;
I want to live in my own fantasy
My death will recreate me once again.

Renunciation can be reincarnation,
Immoral soul want remuneration for living;
Gregarious willpower
Dismaying recovery.

CHAPTER NINETEEN

Dark Fantasy

What darkness expresses?
There is nothing hidden,
Rather than in connected with secrets;
Darkness and emotion coexistent together.

Darkness unmasks the fallacy,
Rainbow failed to masquerade you;
Darkest night writes the brightest story
Self-surrender is called paramountcy.

Dark night, dark room, darkest soul
Your own expectation hurt you;
Vulnerably you expose yourself to it
Your world seems to be very darkest.

But everything begins from here,
Where there is no light;
Darkness absorbs all colors
There is no light without darkness.

It's not an uphill battle
Here one compensates another
There is no joy, no sorrow

There is no life no death.

CHAPTER TWENTY

She Is Alive

I am waiting for the girl
I want to be,
Breaking the paradigm;
What is lifeless.

Who is going to ascertain?
What is right?
When in her life;
There will be no turmoil.

Be brave, be fearless
Not easily manipulated,
Will restrain those;
who are lifeless?

I am going through the corpse
Who died as slave,
Who has no opinion;
who forgot to live the life?

I am invoking the free spirit
To rescue that girl,
She is still alive;

One day she will fearlessly take the stand.

Don't let her past decide her present and future
OH Almighty!!!
Let her be free;
Bring the ferocious girl.

She will become the threat to everyone
People who called her mad,
For being iconoclast;
She will come back to retort them.

In the world of cowards
She is still alive,
She is the power;
She is the Goddess.

CHAPTER TWENTY-ONE

Remembrance

How they have changed everything?
How their ambition
Became fire?
What their ideology was?

The contributions are not meagre
We can't count on fingers
Why we are oblivious?
Ironically their deeds
Has been limited in books.

What had wrenched their heart
For edifying us?
They are now history
we often forget
They are part of us.

Distinctive qualities define personality
Be the change you want to see
Education is what we apply daily
Not for temporary period of time.
Live deliberately!

Our education is our biggest asset
Education is what goes with us
When you go to the deathbed
Nothing we can't take away
what we achieved that is the entity.

CHAPTER TWENTY-TWO

The Return of Goddess

Mother of darkness,
Mother of light;
I invoke you
Please rescue me!!

I know you're with me,
Your pervading presence is everywhere;
You're in the blades of grass
You're in cloud.

You walk with me,
We all come from you;
Please help me to know myself
I am part of yours.

My soul is pure
You're not an abstraction,
You're not an incarnation
You're an ever-present force.

Mother grab my finger
Show me the right path,
Your child is lonely

Only you know how to unleash her.

My journey is very vast
OH wiccan!!
Someone is calling you up,
Give the proof of your existence.

CHAPTER TWENTY-THREE

Wonder women

How she evolved herself?
No need to snowballing it.
What she has suffered,
They don't have the idea about it.
She is hated by many.

How many times she screamed silently?
Nobody can't predict.
But judging her is everyone's cup of tea,
She has had enough;
One day she decided to backfire.

But she still fights
She knows how to take stand for herself,
She uses her anger as a shield;
To protect herself.
She is the Goddess.

Categorized her aggressive and rude is ok!
But she has a child inside her,
Who still craves for caressing and love.
Chocolates and flowers
Her friends forever.

She wants to rule over her emotions
The battle she is fighting with herself,
Often goes unawarded;
Her ambition what kicks her to go forward.
She tries to find out the world in her books.

Her mistakes taught her many lessons
Emotion is her enemy,
Now what she is trying to become;
She is the lonely wolf.
Necessary evil is required.

Who haven't got rescued?
Then she became her own savior,
She is on the way of her own;
No times to love, no time to regret .
She is climbing up the mountain to hunt .

CHAPTER TWENTY-FOUR

Dark Side

Where sunlight doesn't go
Dark temptation,
Grabbed up;
No longer charismatic.

In the absence of sun
Darkness pervading,
Nobody can reach there;
But it's not at all magnificent.

Unconscious mind
creates story,
Creation has lack of creativity;
Throw out it what is not at all worthy.

But darkness has no victory over the lights
Light is here,
Sun light is coming up;
Darkside is engraved by light.

Now there is only light
And it's so glorious,
Now I wake up with the sun;

Want to be bright.

CHAPTER TWENTY-FIVE

The Sound of The Truth

When everywhere there is corruption?
Justice feels throttled,
When the worst remains worst?
People are afraid to raise voice.

The king is roaming naked
But where is the child?
The child is no more,
To raise questions.

Naked king is roaming naked
And protesters are in suffer or graveyard,
The truth is sold out;
On the market of scandalous.

When the basic morality is choked up?
When the kingdom is full of perverts?
Delinquency runs back and forth;
You got stuck in the spin of conspiracy.

Printed by Libri Plureos GmbH in Hamburg,
Germany